Soundprints

Little
Soundprints

Little
Soundprints

Little
Soundprints

Little
Soundprints

Little
Soundprints

P9-DEC-387

Soundprints

Little
Soundprints

Little
Soundprints

Little
Soundprints

Little
Soundprints

Little
Soundprints

2.7
65305

GRAY WOLF PUP'S ADVENTURE

by Stephanie Smith

Illustrated by Robert Hynes

To Judy—S.S.

To my family—R.H.

Book copyright © 2002 Trudy Corporation and the
Smithsonian Institution, Washington DC 20560.

Published by Soundprints Division of Trudy Corporation, Norwalk, Connecticut.

All rights reserved. No part of this book may be reproduced or transmitted in any
form or by any means whatsoever without prior written permission of the publishe

Book design: Marcin D. Pilchowski
Editor: Laura Gates Galvin
Editorial assistance: Chelsea Shriver

First Edition 2002
10 9 8 7 6 5 4 3 2 1
Printed in China

Acknowledgments:
 Our very special thanks to Dr. Don E. Wilson of the Department of System
Biology at the Smithsonian Institution's National Museum of Natural History for h
curatorial review, and our very special thanks to Robert Hynes for his amazing
work under pressure.
 Soundprints would also like to thank Ellen Nanney and Robyn Bissette at
Smithsonian Institution's Office of Product Development and Licensing for their h
in the creation of this book.

Library of Congress Cataloging-in-Publication Data

Smith, Stephanie, 1976-
Gray wolf pup's adventure / by Stephanie Smith ; illustrated by Robert Hynes.
 p. cm.
Summary: A mischievous gray wolf pup strays from his pack and learns a valuab
lesson.
ISBN 1-931465-14-2 (hardcover) — ISBN 1-931465-13-4 (pbk.)
1. Wolves—Juvenile fiction. [1. Wolves—Fiction. 2. Animals—Infancy—Fiction.] I.
Hynes, Robert, ill. II. Title.

PZ10.3.S6548 Gr 2002
[Fic]—dc21

2001049689

Table of Contents

A note to the reader:
Throughout this story you will see words in **bold letters**. There is more information about these words in the glossary. The glossary is in the back of the book.

Chapter 1

ray Wolf Pup's Family

On a sunny day in spring, Gray Wolf Pup and his brothers and sisters are playing outside their **den**. They jump and pounce on each other.

The gray wolf family lives on the **tundra**. The pups' mother sits next to the opening of their den. Other female wolves from the pack sit with her. Together they watch the pups.

Gray Wolf Pup's father is the leader of the **pack**. His father and other males are hunting in their **territory**. Gray Wolf Pup is very big and strong. Someday he will be the leader of a pack.

Gray Wolf Pup is too young to hunt. He and the other wolf pups pretend to hunt. They pounce on each other. They practice for when they are older.

Gray Wolf Pup sees an **ermine** running through the field. The ermine will make a good snack. Gray Wolf Pup is ready to try his first hunt.

Chapter 2

The Chase

Gray Wolf Pup crouches low. He follows the ermine through the field. After a while, he cannot see his brothers and sisters. He has traveled far from the den.

The ermine goes into a small hole in the ground. Gray Wolf Pup stops at the hole. He growls and paws at the hole.

Gray Wolf Pup waits for the ermine to come out. It is getting dark. Gray Wolf Pup is tired of waiting. He looks all around him. Gray Wolf Pup does not know how to get home.

Gray Wolf Pup howls.
He is too far away for
his family to hear him.
Gray Wolf Pup has
never spent a night
away from his pack.

Chapter 3

Pup Is Lost

Gray Wolf Pup is hungry. He sees something moving in the grass. It is a **vole**. The vole runs across the tundra. Gray Wolf Pup crouches low. He quietly follows the vole.

Gray Wolf Pup has never caught his own food. He has watched his father hunt. He knows what to do. He jumps up and pounces on the vole. He has caught his first meal!

Gray Wolf Pup runs.

He stops to howl again.

Soon he hears a howl.

It is not the howl of his

father. The strange howl

comes closer and closer.

Gray Wolf Pup hears sounds around him. It is dark. He can only see yellow eyes looking at him. Then, Gray Wolf Pup sees three big gray wolves. He is in the territory of another pack!

Gray Wolf Pup hears his father's howl! Gray Wolf Pup's father barks at the other wolves. He is telling them to stay away. Gray Wolf Pup runs fast. His father follows. Soon they are safe in their own territory.

Chapter 4

The Big Hunt

Gray Wolf Pup's father barks at him. He is telling him not to leave the pack again. They trot back toward their den with two other wolves from their pack. They see wild sheep asleep in the field.

Gray Wolf Pup follows his father into the field. The sheep will make a good meal for the pack. The wolves surround the sleeping sheep. The sheep wake up. They are scared. They run fast!

One sheep cannot get away. Gray Wolf Pup's father and the other wolves catch the sheep. The wolves enjoy their feast.

At the den, Gray
Wolf Pup runs to his
mother. His mother
barks at him. She
also nuzzles him.
She is happy that
he is safe.

Gray Wolf Pup
is tired. He settles
down to sleep. He
is back in his
home, safe and
sound at last.

Glossary

Den: the place where some animals sleep.

Ermine: a small, short-tailed weasel.

Pack: a group of wolves that lives together

Territory: the area of land on which a wolf pack hunts and lives.

Tundra: an area of northern America that has short grass, small plants, and many rocks. The tundra is very cold.

Vole: a small rodent that resembles a mouse.

Wilderness Facts About the Gray Wolf

Gray wolves live in most of Canada and Alaska. The color of their fur can be black, white, gray, or brown. Full-grown male wolves can weigh from 85 to 115 pounds. Females usually weigh no more than 110 pounds.

Each wolf pack has a leader. The leader is called the *alpha male*. He is the strongest male in the pack. Packs can include two to twelve wolves. Packs usually have parents and two or three litters of pups. There is almost no fighting within the pack. Packs stay in one territory. Males can travel up to 20 miles to hunt for food and bring it back to the den.

Wolves eat moose and caribou. They also eat Dall sheep, Sitka black-tailed deer, mountain goats, and beavers. If larger prey cannot be found, gray wolves will eat voles, snowshoe hares, or squirrels.

Animals that live near gray wolves in the tundra region include:

Arctic foxes	Mountain goats
Black-tailed deer	Reindeer
Caribou	Snowshoe hares
Dall sheep	Snowy owls
Ermines	Voles
Lynx	White-tailed deer

Soundprints

Little
Soundprints

Little
Soundprints

Little
Soundprints

Little
Soundprints

Little
Soundprints

Little
Soundprints

Little